what's your excuse
for not being better
with money

what's your excuse ...

FOR NOT

BEING BETTER WITH MONEY?

Overcome your excuses and get to grips with your personal finance

jo thresher

"There's some very sensible money advice here, with lots of information about how to think about your money as something which supports the life you want and not something that should be feared or revered. Even if you only make a few of the changes suggested in this book it will make you richer and more secure"

Jasmine Birtles, Founder of MoneyMagpie.com

"Jo is a source of great advice and her practical and down to earth approach can't fail to help readers to get to grips with their personal finances"

James Murphy, Founder of The Employee Engagement Alliance

"A great book - Jo mixes motivation, advice and common sense to make personal finance feel manageable and positive. I'd thoroughly recommend this to anyone who wants to improve their own financial situation"

Dr Sam Collins, author and CEO of Aspire

"Jo Thresher makes money accessible and is a breath of fresh air! This book is going to be of real value to many!"

Zoe Sinclair, Director of Employees Matter

"I've always thought that being 'better with money' should be taught in the National Curriculum. I suspect

most people grow up wishing they had better control over their finances. Jo Thresher's book fills the void. It's clearly written and the 'no excuses' format is great at nudging you into developing better money habits – without making you feel too guilty! It's definitely worth spending a bit of pocket money to read it"

Miranda Birch, Miranda Birch Media

"Jo's book is a really fantastic guide in terms of giving a better understanding of money issues and raising awareness of some of the key things that you need to consider when dealing with this very important subject – things which can make the difference between a happy life and a life of anxiety. The book is well written and engaging and I will be recommending it to many of my close friends and family"

Charlotte Knight, MD of trading and digital Game Digital plc

"Jo has an instinctive feel for her subject matter and this book provides a good guide to all of us looking for some common sense advice "

Alex Alway, Brokers CEO's CEO of the year 2015

"Having worked with Jo over the years, I was always so impressed with her enthusiasm to help people. By explaining to employers and individuals how debt can arise and more importantly how quickly debt

can accrue, I believe her contribution to the world in encouraging people to seek help early is really valuable. Jo's new book which is aimed at helping us all be better with money can only add value to our lives"

Karen Thomson MSc FCIPP FHEA, Director at Armstrong Watson

"Jo has a wonderful way of turning the hard-nosed business of managing your money into a practical, every day task. My go-to girl for money tips!"

Lindsay Middleton, Head of Finance Change

"Jo has worked closely with me and my team to devise plans to engage our workforce, and to help them understand their spending habits. She is completely engaging…we have found her help absolutely invaluable; our employees love how Jo is open & honest and we know she genuinely wants to help us to get 'better with money'. Her passion is contagious, she makes us feel there is light at the end of any tunnel"

Michelle Sutton, Payroll & Benefits Manager

Also in this series

What's Your Excuse for not....

Living a Life You Love?
Getting Fit?
Loving Your Job?
Eating Healthily?
Being More Confident?

What's Your Excuse for not Being Better With Money?

This first edition published in 2017 by WYE Publishing
9 Evelyn Gardens, Richmond TW9 2PL
www.wyepublishing.com

Copyright © Jo Thresher 2017

Jo Thresher asserts her moral right to be identified as the author
of this book

ISBN 978-0-9956052-0-6

Printed and bound in Great Britain by
Marston Book Services Ltd, Oxfordshire

Cover and text design by Annette Peppis & Associates

'What's Your Excuse…?' is a UK Registered Trade Mark
(Registration No: 3018995)

www.whatsyourexcuse.co.uk
Follow What's Your Excuse…? on Twitter – @whats_yr_excuse
www.facebook.com/whatsyourexcusebooks

www.betterwithmoney.com
Follow Jo on Twitter – @jothresherjo

Contents

Introduction   17
How this book will help you   19
What being better with money means   21
The consequences of not being better with
    money   24
The benefits of being better with money   26
A note on the limitations of this book   28

The Excuses   29
The past   31
I've always been rubbish with money   31
I've screwed up big time in the past   32
I've been ripped off before   33

Fears   35
What if they go bust?   35
It's all too risky   36
I'll just keep it under the bed   38
If I review my finances I might discover bad news 38

Knowledge   41
The advice online is confusing   41

No one taught me   42
It's all too confusing   42
I don't know where my money goes   43

Home   **45**
My mortgage is the problem   45
My bills just stack up   51
I'll never be able to afford my own home   53

Attitude and beliefs   **55**
Sorting out money is boring   55
I don't want to know   56
People who care too much about money are tight   57
My credit card is my friend   58
I'm worth it   60
I earned it   61
I'm rubbish with money   62
Everyone's in debt   63
I am too young to worry about all this stuff   64

Work and income   **65**
I have no money to manage   65
I have plenty of income, so what if I waste some?   66
I'm not paid enough   67
My income is erratic   68
I don't know what benefits I get from work   70

Outgoings and spending   **75**

I blew the budget on a must-have item   75

My debt is getting out of hand   76

I'm a shopaholic   77

I want to go to the pub   80

I can't help but buy when I see the emails   81

Shopping is therapy   81

I am usually sensible but go mad when I'm
    on holiday   85

I live in my overdraft   85

Food takes up all of my money   86

Shopping is part of my social life   88

I go to the supermarket for milk and spend £30!   90

Financial organisations   **91**

My credit score is rubbish   91

I don't believe in pensions   92

I don't trust banks   94

I hate insurance companies   95

I like to be loyal   97

Tax…argh!   98

My student debt worries me   100

Other people   **103**

My partner/parent does that for me   103

My partner only stays with me for my money   105

I am owed money   106

I have an adviser who sorts out my money   108

Organisation   **111**

I'm so disorganised and the paperwork just
    builds up   111
I lose track of my money   113
I can't find the time to organise my money   114
I know I should get organised but there's always
something that needs my money   115

The future   **117**

I'll never have any money   117
I could be dead tomorrow and you can't take it
    with you   118
My savings are for a rainy day   119
I'm hoping for an inheritance   120

Next Steps   121

Challenge one – income   123
Challenge two – outgoings   124
Challenge three – debt   126
Challenge four – cushions   128
Challenge five – home   129
Challenge six – insurance   131
Challenge seven – pensions   132
Challenge eight – savings   134

Budget Planner   137

Some Final Thoughts   141

About the Author   145

Acknowledgements   147

Reference / Bibliography   149

Index   155

Introduction

How this book will help you

Do you sometimes feel that you could be more in control of your finances? Or do you sometimes feel that your finances are in control of you? Then this book can help. It's aimed at anyone who feels the need to be *better* with money. Not perfect, nor scrooge-like. Its aim is for you to no longer be scared of checking your bank balance, and for you to gain a better understanding of where your money goes. Its aim is that you no longer feel a knot in your stomach when you open your credit card statement. Its aim is that you understand things like interest rates, and that you are no longer confused by pensions, mortgages and tax.

This book addresses all of the common, regular and real excuses which I've heard during nearly thirty years of helping people with their money, which are usually used as reasons not to act or which indicate feelings of helplessness. But you're not helpless, and you *can* act if you understand and tackle those excuses.

You don't need to spend much time managing money when you have a basic budget in place, so I will help with that. And if you have goals and dreams which you can't currently afford, I'll help with planning so that you might be able to afford them in the future.

When you've read this book you'll have a better understanding of where your money comes from and where it goes, new skills to manage that money and a budget plan if you need one. Follow the advice, carry out some basic tasks and then keep doing them – for you, your family and your future.

So are you in? Then let's go.

What being better with money means

Being better with money is about being better with life. To *live* we need a certain amount of money, unless we are going to camp in the woods and live on berries. To have a *life,* if you know what you want to experience and enjoy and what your purpose is, you will need more money. This is the difference between *living* and enjoying *life.*

Happiness isn't necessarily about money. I have met very unhappy rich people and very happy people who would be considered poor by many. So what does *rich* look like for you? What does rich mean to you? Is it even the right word for your financial goals? What is your word and what does it mean to you? What objectives and goals do you have and what do you need to organise or understand in order to reach them? A notepad may be useful for this process, and in fact for dealing with money in general. That way you will remember what you need to do, why you are doing it and how far you have come. I am a big fan of making notes and creating reminders to take action and I will remind you to do this throughout this book.

Start by writing down what *rich* (or your own word)

looks like to you – it doesn't have to be a list, you could draw a picture – and discuss with a partner or friend. The things most of us value and enjoy do not normally need millions of pounds.

Next, consider what feeling better about money would be like.

Draw five circles and pop in the words which come to mind when you think about money.

Rate your level of money happiness from 1 to 10.

This should give you a starting point and some clarity about the money issues you need to address. You can now work on those and put a plan in place to push your money happiness rating up and achieve your objectives.

Being better with money will improve your happiness, your relationships and your future, but if you're stuck for your own personal objectives, here are some common benefits of being better with money:

- I won't be constantly worrying
- I will know where I stand financially
- If there is an emergency I will have some cash to deal with it
- I will not fear the postman
- I will open my bills when they arrive
- I will not be overdrawn
- I will have some savings
- I will understand my mortgage

- My health won't suffer due to financial worries
- My relationships will be better
- I will be able to make choices based on what I want, not what I can afford
- I will have a plan for reducing my debt
- I will understand my pension
- My family will be better off
- I will be able to buy that thing I have wanted forever
- I will be out of debt
- I'll prove to people that I could do it
- I will be able to afford to change jobs
- I'll have some savings for retirement
- I will focus on what's important
- I can stop comparing myself to others
- I can help my kids learn about money
- I will feel good about myself
- I'll be able to make plans for the future
- I'll know that I have overcome my excuses!

Use your own personal objectives and this list as motivation to take control of your money and if you find yourself struggling at any point use them as a reminder of why it's so important to work on being *better with money*.

The consequences of not being better with money

Currently in Great Britain 21.8 million adults are not confident that they are saving enough for a rainy day. In July 2015 StepChange Debt Charity reported that if every household in Great Britain saved £1,000 it would reduce the number of households in problem debt by 500,000.[1] That's half a million families who would be saved from the pain and stress of money problems. We need to save.

Money problems cause relationship breakdowns, employment troubles, health issues, business problems and even, tragically, death. In 2015 academics at Bristol University estimated that 1,000 extra deaths from suicide and an additional 30–40,000 suicide attempts may

1   StepChange Debt Charity, Becoming a Nation of Savers
https://www.stepchange.org/Portals/0/documents/Reports/
BecominganationofsaversStepChangeDebtCharityreport.pdf

have occurred following the economic slump in 2008.[2]

This is why making yourself financially resilient is so important, not just for you but for your partner, loved ones and family.

What does it mean for you to not feel in control of your money, and therefore your life?

Have you made decisions based on your financial situation? Have you ever thought, 'I have to stay in this job/marriage/industry/area because of my debt/over-draft/pension/lack of knowledge about money?' That's not good news. Money should *enable* not *disable* you. So if all of this scary stuff is resonating with you and you want things to change for the better, you need to start taking small steps towards where you want to be.

If you haven't already made some notes as suggest-ed in the previous chapter, spend time now deciding what being financially fit means to you. This is different for all of us but it's important that you are clear on this. You can then use the advice, tips and challenges in this book to take control and improve your situation.

---

2   David Gunnell, Jenny Donovan, Maria Barnes, Rosie Davies, Keith Hawton, Nav Kapur, Will Hollingworth, Chris Metcalfe, The 2008 Global Financial Crisis: effects on mental health and suicide http://www.bris.ac.uk/media-library/sites/policybristol/documents/ PolicyReport-3-Suicide-recession.pdf See also https://www.theguardian.com/society/2015/nov/12/austerity-a-factor-in-rising-suicide-rate-among-uk-men-study

The benefits of being better with money

As I've already mentioned, the definition of being better with money is very personal. It's also a journey depending on where you are starting from. It is dependent on your lifestyle, your age, your job and many other factors. But in another way it isn't. If you are earning and you have bills, there are some standard, basic money management tasks from which you will benefit.

How many of these features of being better with money can you tick off?

- More income than outgoings – put simply, spare money at the end of the month
- A financial plan – a clear idea of where you're going with your money and why
- Minimal, manageable, 'good', cheap debt only – for things you need and which bring you reward
- A day to day plan – a system for your spending, bills and saving
- Minimised outgoings – not giving away your hard-earned money when you don't need to

- An emergency fund – so that money is not the issue if something unexpected happens
- Money for what makes you happy – a pot for your development or happiness
- Plans for the future – plans for your mortgage, your retirement and your dependents
- A positive financial outlook – less fear, more understanding

This book will help with the ones you haven't ticked!

A note on the limitations of this book

This book is intended to provide techniques, tips and tools and to help you improve your financial situation, but it does not constitute personal financial advice. Every individual's financial situation is unique so if you are unsure about any investment or financial decision you should seek expert independent advice, as the author and publisher cannot accept liability if things go wrong.

This book is aimed at readers in the UK.

The Excuses

The past

I've always been rubbish with money

So when you were born the midwife said, 'Here's another one who is going to be rubbish with money!' Except she didn't. Stuff happened along the way. Your upbringing, family, school, religion, where you live, friends, good things, bad things: these have all influenced how you feel about money and how good you are at managing it. This is all below the surface but nonetheless it influences every money decision you make.

So what is your earliest money memory? The one you remember best may not be the earliest, but it may have shaped you a little along the way. It can be worth thinking about how your parents or caregivers dealt with money. Were they organised? Did they fight? Were they careful or extravagant? If something like a divorce or bereavement happened and changed the family finances, did that change your thinking? Some of this thinking might be a little hard. You may benefit from talking to somebody about how you feel, perhaps a friend or a professional. You are not alone. The thoughts and feelings you are having about money are very common.

Fortunately the past doesn't have to dictate the future. Think of money like you'd think of your health and fitness. Being healthier and fitter needs a plan – for instance, to go shopping for healthier food, to buy some new trainers for the gym, choosing which exercise to do, when to do it and where. It's exactly the same with money. If you haven't thought about it and planned before, or had any support along the way, it will take a little time to shift the negative feelings, much like burning fat or gaining muscle. Use the past to help you learn for the future and then use the appropriate challenges at the back of this book.

> The past doesn't have to dictate the future

I've screwed up big time in the past

I did once, at 17, when Barclays kindly gave me a payment card and an overdraft and I gave all the money I didn't have to Topshop and Miss Selfridge! I then went on to realise that if you don't pay all of your bills on time, debt will accumulate. Getting a loan to pay off that debt and then going on a holiday which I couldn't afford was not one of my finest moments either. One

January morning at about the age of 20 this all came home to roost. A huge pile of envelopes was staring at me, I knew the bills couldn't be ignored anymore, there was no more credit and I had to face facts. I was terrified. But I made a decision to get it sorted and to *never ever feel that fear again*.

So firstly, where are you now? Is the debt paid off? If it's not, see "My debt is getting out of hand".

If it is paid off, well done! Be proud. I am sure it wasn't easy. So what now? We need to make sure you have the skills and confidence to never let this happen again. So can I be a bit personal? Why did it happen? Were you young, foolish and uneducated about money? Was it a relationship breakdown, gambling or addictions, or trusting someone you shouldn't have? I am sorry if thinking about it is painful but understanding what happened will ensure it doesn't happen again. Would it help to write it down? Forgive yourself and, if appropriate, others. Then write down how you will ensure it doesn't happen again.

I've been ripped off before

Did you feel stupid? Did you feel angry? Good. Remember that feeling and use it to stop it happening again.

Are you familiar with the saying, 'Fool me once shame on you, fool me twice shame on me'? A bad thing happened. You had your fingers burnt. But if you acknowledge why it happened – lack of time, lack of understanding, greed, not checking things out – you can ensure it won't happen again.

Learning more about money will mean this is far less likely to happen again. Yes, there are bad people out there but checking out your rights, acting a little slower and asking a few more questions will mean that you are less likely to be ripped off again.

Fears

What if they go bust?

Most everyday mainstream financial products have protection built in, in case the organisation goes bust. This means your money is protected in the event of an organisation not being able to meet its liabilities.

But you should always understand who regulates your product, and where you stand.

For example, if your bank, building society or credit union goes bust at the time of writing you would be entitled to compensation through the Financial Services Compensation Scheme up to a maximum of £75,000 per account in the same banking group. To ensure that you get the maximum benefit from this, check out how this covers any joint accounts and if you have money with two banks in the same banking group. Check the Financial Conduct Authority's website for advice.[3] Make sure you know the answer to the question, 'What

Understand who regulates your product

---

3   https://www.the-fca.org.uk/consumers/claim-compensation-firm-fails

happens if this company goes bust?'

If you invest in products linked to a market return – such as shares or units in a pension, the above protection scheme will *not* stop you losing your money if the investment goes down in value. So you should choose carefully where your money is invested and take into account when you might want to access that money. Read on to "It's all too risky" for more on this.

It's all too risky

What do you think is the risk? If you're worried about a bank or investment company going bust, see "What if they go bust?" above. But if you're worried about an investment going down in value, read on.

We would all love to invest or save our money where it has a high return (it goes up in value) and low risk (the possibility of it going down in value) but frankly, if someone promises you this, be suspicious!

Finding the right savings account or investment product would be easy if you had a crystal ball but you don't so you need to weigh up the risks against the potential gains. Understand where your money is invested and what could happen. For example, a bank account is cash kept by the bank for easy access and which does not go down in value. However, if you've invested in shares or equities (they are the same thing) there is a risk that they will fall in value as the price normally varies daily. So understanding the different risks to your money and what they mean for you is important.

There are many factors to consider but here are some to help you work out how much risk you want to take on:

- The purpose of your investment
- Your circumstances and whether you can afford to lose money
- When you will need the money (flexibility and certainty)
- Your understanding and knowledge
- Costs, fees and value for money
- Performance (against benchmarks)
- Legislative and market changes (for instance to your tax position or ISA allowances)

Be realistic and do your research. If a product sounds too complicated or risky, or you don't understand it, find an alternative with which you are happy and which you do understand.

Risk is a fact of life, but understanding and making informed decisions on how much exposure to it you are willing to take on can put you in control.

I'll just keep it under the bed

Firstly, well done for having some money saved somewhere! I also understand why the risk of being defrauded bothers you. Financial fraud is growing at an alarming rate. However, if you take simple steps to protect yourself and examine closely anything related to your finances, you will avoid most fraud. On the flip side, all the financial savvy in the world cannot prevent you being burgled or having someone come into your home and take your money, if that's where you store it. You will also miss out on earning interest and be adversely affected by inflation.

Taking into account the lack of interest, the reduction in your buying power over time and the risk of theft it makes more sense to find a safer place to put your money.

Take a look at the two chapters above for more reassurance.

If I review my finances I might discover bad news

Maybe, maybe not. What does *bad* mean to you? If it's not being able to cover your bills, you need to take action. If it's having large debts, you also need to take action. You can't take action unless you *know* what your financial situation is, and if the answer is bad you need to stop it getting worse.

What if you are made redundant at nine o'clock tomorrow? If you don't know where you stand financially the worry would be very bad. But if you knew you had an emergency fund and your bills under control you could throw your energy into winning a new job. Less panic, more energy.

Have you enough savings? What is enough to you? Have you set a goal? How about writing it down? Know where you are going with your money and why it is important.

So what is *bad* for you and, more importantly, what is *good*?

Knowing what good looks like, knowing how you can flex your budget and knowing the safety net you have for rainy days is empowering. Check out the challenges at the end of this book for help, and start one today.

Knowledge

The advice online is confusing

The internet is massive. Which is great when you are looking for pictures of cute kittens but trickier when looking for help with money.

Firstly, be clear on what you are trying to find, then start with the relevant regulator or advice site. Currently a good place to start is the Money Advice Service.[4] This government backed site is there to give advice and explanations on all financial matters. I also recommend MoneySavingExpert.com.[5] Martin Lewis started this site with the aim of helping consumers. Don't just browse the highlighted shopping deals though; go there for the latest bank rates, credit cards with low interest rates, up to date mortgage deals and lots of other great help and information.

> Be clear on what you are trying to find

If you stick with official regulators' sites or well-established and well-respected sites you won't go far

---

4   www.moneyadviceservice.org.uk
5   www.moneysavingexpert.com

wrong. I've included a number of the most useful websites at the end of this book.

No one taught me

I agree that we aren't taught money management at school, and what's the point of knowing algebra or the chemical symbol for carbon but not how mortgages work? I hear you.

So you need to learn. The earlier you get this stuff sorted, the sooner you will be able to tackle problems, build a cushion and be happier and more comfortable. Use the challenges and recommended websites at the back of this book to get started.

It's all too confusing

It may be confusing because it's not organised.

So let's start with one thing at a time. Open your purse or wallet. What's in there? A mass of receipts, store cards and loyalty cards mixed in with the money? Or is it neatly laid out with a shopping list, and a credit card for emergencies only? This is your 'money' you carry with you daily. Each item needs to have a purpose.

So what is the cash for? What are the cards for? What are you going to spend today? Do you have a plan for today's spending? Plan it, do it, review it. Not so confusing now?

Plan it, do it, review it

You can apply the same approach to all aspects of your finances – take stock, plan, carry out the plan and review. Take a look at the challenges at the back of this book for help.

I don't know where my money goes

Was it stolen by the fairies?! Or was it that latte this morning, that lunch and bottle of water or that magazine and ready meal you bought on the way home? If you're not sure, try keeping a spending log. Get a receipt for everything and I mean *everything*! If you don't get a receipt, write it on an envelope and put all of your receipts in it. Then add them up. Now you understand where your money goes, which is great progress.

Write on each receipt if it was:

- Essential
- Something which you could have bought for less
- Something you didn't need

The lesson from the 'could have bought for less' items should be obvious, and it's down to you to shop around. Whatever you've identified as 'didn't need' took money which could have been saved for something else. You should be able to see how you can start reducing your outgoings.

There might be some difficult things to face here. Grab your notebook, consider what you want to change. Write it down and write down how you're going to make the change. Do it.

Analyse your bills too. Are you paying too much for your energy? Could you get a smart meter? Have you checked your phone bill? Reviewed your car and house insurance? Look at every bill, line by line. Can you reduce them? Any money saved can help reduce debt, increase savings or fund those things you've always wanted to do!

Home

My mortgage is the problem

The UK has become a nation of home owners, or aspiring home owners, and this demand for property, particularly in our big cities has caused property prices to rise. Depending on where you are on the property ladder this could be good news or it could cause you problems. The people of some nations, such as Switzerland and Germany, do not own generally their own homes and see our obsession with property ownership as strange; but we now see our home as a part of our retirement plan, or as an asset to pass on to our children, not just a place to live. This is a lot to ask from a mortgage or home, but we all need a home.

When did you last review your mortgage rate?

So let's look at how you can keep your mortgage manageable. (If you don't yet own a home but want to, see "I'll never be able to afford my own home").

Firstly, when did you last review your mortgage rate? As I write we are still in a period of very low interest rates but that doesn't mean you are on the lowest rate you can get. However, since the UK government's mortgage review in April 2015, the way lenders decide how much they will lend you has changed. It is no longer simply a multiple of your salary. Many other factors are taken into account. So see "I am worried about my credit score" before you do anything.

Secondly, are your finances in order? A lender will want to see that you can still afford this mortgage and is likely to ask for your bank statements, full details of income and outgoings, and will definitely check your credit/debt position. If necessary, use the challenges at the end of this book to help prepare for approaching potential lenders. Every single item is now important to them. So if your regular manicure or pub visit is shown on your bank statement, and you don't include it on your list of outgoings, it could affect who will lend to you.

Thirdly, how long are you staying in this property? Are you thinking of moving, downsizing, changing job or location? Are you planning a bigger family? Or have the kids left home and you would be happy to have fewer rooms to clean? Remortgaging can be costly, so you should consider these questions seriously. Balancing the cost of remortgaging with any change in circumstances is important. Can you still afford to live in the home you are in? Emotional attachments aside, would a cheaper home be more suitable? Should you think outside the box? Take Stacy, who decided to create her very own Narnia by moving her parents, grandma and in-laws into one big property, saving lots of money. Now this may be a bit extreme for some but it works for Stacy. I'm not sure I could live with my mother-in-law, or if she'd want to live with me, but it's an example of taking an unconventional approach to solving the problem of affording a mortgage. What unconventional approaches could you try?

Next, are you clear on the type of mortgage you have currently and your plan to repay it? Here are the options:

Repayment mortgages

You pay part interest (the cost of borrowing the money) and part capital (what you owe) each month. This means what you owe (the capital) goes down a little each month and therefore, assuming the interest rate stays the same, the interest part of your payment goes down too. So you owe less, meaning that as time goes on more of what you pay each month pays off what you owe. Don't get too excited by this – it sounds good, but it's normal for this to take twenty five years!

These mortgages give you a great opportunity to save money: if you overpay, either slightly or up to the annual overpayment limit, you will reduce your capital more quickly. Most lenders do have a maximum amount you can repay each year, so check this out with your current and any potential new lenders. There are some great calculators online[6] that demonstrate how, by paying a little extra, your loan will be paid off a few years earlier. In this era of very low interest rates, paying off more of the mortgage is great for two reasons – should rates rise, you are already comfortable with a higher payment and you will simply owe less.

Interest only mortgages

This type of product was oversold for a period of time as it is cheaper than the above method. You pay interest on the capital (the amount you owe) and therefore what you owe does not go down. You then have to set up a plan for paying off the capital at the end of the term. Many people had savings plans called endowments for this purpose, and unfortunately a lot of these forecasted much higher returns than they delivered, hence their bad reputation now. Other products which can be used to pay off the capital are pensions, ISAs or shares. Another option is to downsize, relying on an increase in the value of your home. This can work, but not if you need to downsize during a recession or property crisis.

Having a plan for repaying your interest only

---

6   Try these:
https://www.moneyadviceservice.org.uk/en/tools/mortgage-calculator
http://www.moneysavingexpert.com/mortgages/mortgage-rate-calculator

mortgage is vital to being debt free in later life. You can still pay off part of the mortgage regularly, or annually, but you are likely to have a limit to what can be repaid. If you have this type of mortgage what is your plan to repay? Again, there are some great calculators online[7] to help you work out a plan.

Offset mortgages

Your mortgage and savings are held with the same organisation and you are only charged interest on the combined balance. These can be repayment or interest only, and rules will be specific to your deal.

And if you're not clear on how interest rates work?

Fixed interest

Your interest rate will be fixed for a specific period of time – a good bet for those who like certainty, as you can budget for a known amount, or if you think rates are about to rise due to economic changes, but not so good if the interest rate falls. It's likely that you'd have to pay an early repayment charge if you wanted to switch deals or lenders before the fixed term ended.

---

7   *Try this one:*
https://www.moneyadviceservice.org.uk/en/tools/mortgage-calculator

Variable

The rate you pay on a variable mortgage will be decided by your mortgage lender so there is less predictability. If the Bank of England base rate went up by 1% your lender could choose to do nothing or increase its own rates by more or less than 1%. In fact your lender could increase or decrease their variable rate at any time.

On a variable rate mortgage you won't normally have to pay an early repayment charge if you want to pay off your mortgage early or remortgage to a new deal.

Capped

Your rate will not go above a certain amount. Again, good for those who like certainty. Early repayment charges may apply so check with your lender or potential new lenders.

When you've considered mortgage rates and repayment amounts, it's important to understand what rate changes might mean. For instance, for every £100,000 of capital owed, a rate rise of 0.25% would mean an increase of £20.83 per month. A rise of 0.5% would mean an extra £41.66. Can you afford that? If so, why not pay that extra amount off your mortgage each month to pay it off more quickly? Or save it somewhere else. If you wouldn't be able to afford that or can't afford your mortgage now, and can't find a better deal, use the challenges at the back of the book to take control of your money and identify how you might be able to reorganise your finances so you can afford it.

My bills just stack up

If you deal with them when they arrive they won't stack up, but this takes a bit of organisation. Do you need a visual reminder of what's due to be paid? Would a list in your purse or wallet help, or a spreadsheet? If dealing with them when they arrive sounds too daunting, how about setting aside a day per week to deal with them?

Setting up monthly budgeted direct debits for your utility bills would ensure that you don't have nasty big bills, and most companies will let you choose when in the month you pay. The closer this is to pay day the quicker your money is out of your account before you can spend it on other things.

If the bills are for credit card spending and the amount you've spent always comes as a surprise, now is the time to *ditch* them. Credit cards are great for those that can plan spending and utilise interest free deals, and for real emergencies. For the rest of us they are hugely bad news and mean we spend money we don't have, on stuff we don't need, earning huge profits for the companies behind them. Start to pay with cash and check your balance regularly. Use the 'money pots' method, which you'll find in "I lose track of my money" and really think about how you will feel when you're still paying for something in years to come (and yes it will be years if you only pay minimum payments).

Imagine you were not allowed any credit at all for a whole month. Could you manage? That's my challenge to you. I am not saying you need to pay all your debt off immediately, but start by not accumulating any more.

There is a real pride in getting things under control. After attending one of my debt management workshops, Michelle contacted me to say that she was now back in the black and had not gone overdrawn for the first time in many years. We talked about how she felt and she said she felt happy and *proud*. We noted how it seems easier to get further into debt when you already have debt. She said that now she has it under control, her big plan is to stay proud.

If you want to experience this pride you can start small. For instance one thing which helped Michelle was simply not going shopping. She said she just didn't go into town and instead did lots of other things she needed to do. What can you do to avoid spending and creating more bills so that you can start feeling proud?

I'll never be able to afford my own home

If owning your own home is important to you, you'll need to get serious about it. Getting on the property ladder is not a piece of cake, but it can be done. The government now offers many (actually very good) schemes to help you get on the ladder. They change regularly, and many people are not aware of them. Make sure you're not missing out by finding out more on the Help to Buy website[8]. Also contact your local authority, housing associations and home builders to ask what they can offer.

Work out what you need for a deposit and put together a plan to build it up. My own first home was the result of me having a day job *and* an evening job and selling anything I didn't need. My Christmas present was money to pay conveyancing fees! It took two years but I have never regretted those extra hours and can't even remember what I sold. Write down your top three actions for getting the money you need and then make a start on them.

---

8   *https://www.helptobuy.gov.uk*

Attitude and beliefs

Sorting out money is boring

Sometimes yes, sometimes no. If sorting out money means you can go on a lovely holiday would it still be boring? If spending time on your finances means that the pile of paper on the counter doesn't give you a sick feeling in your stomach, would that make you happier?

What would it mean for you to feel in control of your finances, or be debt free? Sorting out your money can mean you feel more relaxed – is feeling better boring?

Do you need an incentive to do it? What about setting a goal that if you can save yourself a certain amount of money you will start to save for that thing you would love to own or do?

Start with a simple review of where your money goes – see "I don't know where my money goes" for help.

I don't want to know

What would you do if a stranger stuck his hand in your pocket, grabbed £20 and wandered off? You would shout! You would feel robbed! You would act.

This is probably happening to you weekly. If you have old pension plans with high charges, if you are paying more than you need for gas or electricity or if you bought something and didn't shop around. But that's ok. You don't want to know. You're happy that companies make money from you. You don't want to know. Companies get richer while you get a sinking feeling in your stomach when your bills and statements arrive. You don't want to know. Or do you?

Give away as little of your money as possible

I would suggest a healthy aim is to give away as little of your money as possible to organisations, meaning that you can choose where your money goes. A little passion or anger about where your money goes will give you some energy to sort this out.

For example, could you reduce your bank charges? This might mean you could save £5 per month. Have you been meaning to set up a regular payment to a charity? Who would you rather have the money – bank or charity?

People who care too much about money are tight

So you would prefer to be super generous? Frivolous even? Unless you have money to give away, knowing how to handle money and what you have to spend gives you power not fear. It doesn't make you mean, it gives you the freedom to be happier.

As a manager of people am I more impressed by the person who has the latest gadget or fancy car, who throws money around or the person who quietly mentions his plan to get his first home by budgeting carefully?

Who is impressed by people throwing money around?

Who *is* impressed by people throwing money around? You? Do you want to be the person who appears to be rich and who is always first at the bar? Well, how would a person become that way? If they are genuinely wealthy how did that happen? Probably not through being carefree about money. If they are not rich they may be racking up debt, which isn't clever.

Think of yourself and your money like a business. Will you be profitable at the end of this year? Will your 'business' suffer if you don't keep a tight rein on expenses or bills?

Caring about your financial wellbeing will always serve you well. If you want to have frivolous moments, allowing yourself a set amount of 'treat' money could work better for you. This money could be in a special account, pot or envelope. Know that you have budgeted for a treat and that it's not going to hurt you financially to spend it.

My credit card is my friend

It might be, it might not. Do you pay it off every month without going overdrawn or taking out a loan? Do you get some sort of cashback reward? Then it's your friend.

Alternatively, if you only pay the minimum payment every month, or only a little over the minimum, do you know how much interest you are paying? If you only pay minimum payments on a credit card balance of £5000, with 20% APR, it will take almost 32 years to pay off! However if you paid a fixed amount of £100 it would take 8 years, a quarter of the time. So think carefully about the monthly payments you are making.

For cards taken out after 1st April 2011 the minimum payment must always cover fees, interest and charges plus 1% of the amount you owe. However on older credit cards minimum monthly repayments can be set at very low levels, sometimes as low as 2%. If you only make the minimum repayment on these your debt could take decades to pay off and in that time you could pay thousands of pounds in interest.

As you can see credit cards could be your enemy and it might be worth changing the way you view this sort of debt so that you can reduce and eventually get rid of it to ensure a happier future. What could you do with that extra money? Believe you can get out of debt and you will. Can you move this debt to an interest free card? Is there a lower rate out there? Then work out a repayment plan. The Money Advice Service offers a useful online calculator to help you with this[9].

> Credit cards could be your enemy

Credit cards can be really useful, but unless you are really disciplined they will bite back. Using them for emergencies only is great, but it may be better to have an emergency savings fund instead. Then you don't have to pay interest on an emergency which could push you into a debt spiral.

---

9   https://www.moneyadviceservice.org.uk/en/tools/credit-card-calculator

I'm worth it

Yes, you are worth it, as one of the cleverest advertisement campaigns ever keeps telling us. But worth what? Worth spending £40 on the latest beauty product? How does that work? Because *you're* worth it a company gets your hard-earned cash? When did we start equating ourselves with products or items, most of which we use up or throw away?

I think an 'I'm worth it' mind set really has nothing to do with money. It's about how you feel about yourself – do you deserve or merit the item you want to buy? This is advertising at its greatest – it has twisted your thinking so you now weigh up if you are worth a *thing*. If you believe you are you buy the item but if in the back of your mind on a darker, downbeat day you think you aren't, you buy it anyway! You rebel against the feeling of not deserving or being worth

Can you really measure your own worth in stuff?

it and so prove that feeling wrong! Stop for a minute – can you really measure your own worth in *stuff*? No you can't, and stuff won't fix your feelings for long.

You don't deserve to waste money on things which will bring you only a few moments of happiness, and which may then make you resentful as you think, 'Why did I waste that money?'

Try this: think of someone you love very much. Now think of all the stuff you have bought on impulse because you believed you deserved it. Which matters more, the loved one or the stuff? When you weigh up stuff versus other more meaningful things it is *just stuff*.

So do not go shopping with 'worth it' in your mind. Do something that *is* worth your time and money instead.

I earned it

Perhaps you have heard yourself say, 'I have earned it, I have worked hard all week, I haven't been out, I am tired, it's been a nightmare with the weather/kids/traffic, I earned this thing'.

Let's back up. What does your employer pay you? That's what you *earn*. You then make a choice about what you buy with those hard-earned pounds. You can *earn* approval, trust or confidence from others but you don't earn stuff unless you win it in a game show.

So perhaps you're thinking, 'I work hard, I have earned the right to spend my money on this item'. Well, if you do have spare cash for this and really want it, can you get it more cheaply somewhere else? And calculate how many hours of work it will take to earn this item. Take your salary after tax, divide it by 52 then by the number of hours you work each week. The resulting figure is the amount you earn per hour. Now calculate how many hours you will have to work to earn the money for the item you're planning to buy. Do you still want it?

If you don't actually have the spare cash for what you believe you've earned, buying it is going to push you into debt and it will cost you far more, which you really don't deserve.

I'm rubbish with money

All the time? Make a list. Write down the times you've been good with money and the times you've been bad then try to learn from these. Are you more disciplined when you have too little money? Or are you good with your employer's money but not with your own? Or is it something else? Too much money spent on nights out but you budget well for bills? Are unexpected expenses a problem but you save for holidays? You should be able to see a particular area you would like to improve and you can use the challenges at the back of this book to help you do that.

Everyone's in debt

There are different types of debt and understanding this is important. Good debt is a mortgage, a loan to purchase a car to get to work, or to fund education costs, or credit cards paid off every month. Bad debt is credit cards, overdrafts, loans, HP, pawn broker borrowing and payday loans which you cannot afford to pay off, or debt which doesn't add value to your overall financial position.

Why is this distinction important? Well, a mortgage and an affordable loan to buy a car enhance your life, other debts don't. Be clear on whether you are taking on good debt or bad and acknowledge that just because you have some good debt for good reason, it doesn't mean you have to take on unnecessary debt.

Be clear on whether you are taking on good debt or bad

On the subject of car loans, do you really need a fancy expensive car which will only depreciate? Think carefully and do lots of planning and research on finance for things like car buying, *before* you go to the showroom! I cannot state that enough. You wouldn't buy a car from a bank so don't buy debt from a garage. Research the best loans, compare APRs and work out how long any loan will take to pay back.

Note that student debt in the UK is slightly different – see "I have student debt" for more on this.

I am too young to worry about all this stuff

You're never too young to think about money. Getting to grips with money is a life-skill you *need*. Yes it might mean you feel a little more mature, but if that means you can afford a holiday, a car or a home surely that's a good thing? The better you are at managing your finances the more likely you are to be happy, to sleep better and to afford more fun!

You can be the architect of a great future, or make your financial journey difficult. If someone had taken 10% of every penny you had ever been given and squirrelled it away for you, would you be happy with the nest egg you now had? Would you have noticed that you had £9 pocket money instead of £10? Or imagine your employer took 10% of your salary every month and saved it for you? Could you have managed without that 10%? The earlier you start saving the more money you'll have for the future.

Work and income

I have no money to manage

In my experience the less money someone has the better they are at budgeting. Yet sometimes life treats you badly, sometimes it tricks you and sometimes the best choices aren't available to lower earners. But checking you are managing your money in the best possible way is important, no matter what you earn.

A friend of mine didn't realise her bank account carried a monthly fee of £15. This was the difference between her being able to afford a school trip for her daughter and not. Properly examining her outgoings led her to identifying this.

Are there opportunities for more income? Check if there is a state benefit available to you. Could you rent out a room, sell stuff you don't need or make things to sell? Look into switching bank accounts to get a financial incentive (if your credit rating allows, check it out before you apply), pet sit, baby sit, do some ironing for someone. There are thousands of ideas online.[10]

---

10   Try these:
http://www.moneysavingexpert.com
http://www.moneymagpie.com

Do be careful of any idea that looks too good to be true, as it normally will be, and anything which requires an upfront payment from you should be triple-checked.

I have plenty of income, so what if I waste some?

Great, I'm pleased for you, and if you are that 1 in 14,000,000 lottery winner then feel free to put this book down now! Come back when you have spent it all.

If you're not a multi-millionaire do you really have everything you need in place? For instance, are you protected if something goes wrong? Check out your insurance policies. Ensure that you and your family are protected in the event of an emergency, ill health, job loss or death. Look forward and ensure you will have enough to live on not only now but in the future. If you really are flush but some of your money is being spent on banking charges, interest or products which you throw away, what better use could that money be put to? Have an understanding of where your money goes, your assets and your liabilities before you allow yourself to 'waste' money now.

I'm not paid enough

Is your employer genuinely paying you less than the market rate? If so have you spoken to them about this and demonstrated why you deserve to be paid more? Also consider whether, if they increased the pay for everyone doing the same job as you, they would still be able to keep the business afloat.

Can you do more in your current role to earn more? Do you have a career development plan which will result in you earning more? If not, start one. You might need some self-development money so make sure you include that in your budget. Also check if your current employer will help out with the cost of training or exams. Imagine, that mean old employer might help prepare you for your next step! Even if they won't pay for training will they give you paid time to learn from another colleague or to attend courses?

Could you take on another part-time job which could grow into a full-time job and replace your current one? Have you considered a portfolio career, where you use different skills, doing different things (including hobbies) to earn money. The world of work is so much more flexible with modern technology.

If there is a pay gap between you and others doing the same job for another company, how about applying for a job at that company? Or are your colleagues, com-

mute and familiarity with your role worth more than the
potential increase in income?

Consider what's important to you in the balance
between your job, career prospects, money and time.
Put a daily price on your happiness, work/life balance,
comfort and security. Try this calculation:

Current salary + benefits + time + commute + value of
familiarity
vs
New salary + benefits + time + new commute + advan-
tages of change of role

You should now know whether you're happy to stay
where you are on your current salary or whether you
should be planning to move on.

My income is erratic

Are you a freelancer, temporary worker, project-based
contractor or on commission? As a business owner I
am familiar with the feeling of being flush with income
one month and struggling with very little the next. The
problem is that your bills and outgoings are broadly
similar from month to month.

We all fool ourselves when we receive a windfall or bonus. Take Paul, 'When I get my bonus I am going to buy the latest big screen TV!' Only he's forgotten that he's already told his partner it would pay for their summer holiday, which has already been booked. Plus his bank account is already a little overdrawn this month….

This is what can get us into difficulty when we're not in receipt of regular income. It's not simply that our pay is erratic, it's our 'double spending' and lack of planning.

How could Paul, or you, do it better? It's really important to work out what you have going out daily, weekly, monthly and yearly, also the potential one-off expenses such as car tax, tyres, events and emergencies. Hence, if Paul knows January is a quiet month but his car will need its MOT in February and his bonus is not due until March, he can plan accordingly. There is a simple budget planner which you can use at the end of this book.

What else? Knowing what you need as a bare minimum is vital too. Once the bills are paid, you can then allocate remaining cash for the leaner months.

Let's look at Louise. She has a regular salary which covers 90% of her bills but needs her monthly incentive payments to top up and for savings and holidays. However if an emergency happens in the wrong month it can throw her off balance. Clearly Louise cannot predict when emergencies will happen, so when she gets a big incentive payment she needs to set aside some of that for an emergency fund. How much do you need in an emergency fund?

Finally, ask yourself if, when you do have money, you splurge? Before you allow yourself a shopping trip bear in mind the advice above and make sure you've got future outgoings covered and emergency funds topped up before you start spending!

I don't know what benefits I get from work

Workplace benefits are actually *free money*. So find out what your employer gives you for free.

Here's a guide to what you might be given:

Life cover/death in service

This is often shown as a multiple of your salary. So if your cover offers 4 x salary, somebody you have nominated will benefit from 4 x your salary if you die. It's not for you, as you will have to die for that person to receive it, but the good news is that you don't have to die in the office or during working hours for the benefit to be paid. If you receive this benefit, keep your nomination form up to date. This means it can be paid out really quickly if the worst happens, to the correct person.

And if you do have this benefit calculate if it would be enough to protect your loved ones or dependents after your death. You may still need to buy more cover privately.

Pensions

Yes, I know, boring, but don't fall asleep! Pensions are important and simple to understand – they are the money you will rely on when you stop working. Understanding the type of pension you get from your employer is important. Find out what your employer will match. For example, if you pay 3% of salary, they might match it. But if you pay more, they might pay more, so understand what is on offer here and take full advantage of it.

See also "I don't believe in pensions" and the Pensions challenge at the end of this book.

Healthcare plans

These are normally known as private medical plans or even 'BUPA' (which is just one of the market leaders in this area). These plans provide for you to receive certain medical treatments on a private basis, often meaning quicker treatment, at a time of your choice, in a clinic or hospital of your choice. They tend to get used more and therefore more expensive the older you get.

You may have an 'excess' on a plan, which means that if you make a claim you will have to contribute an agreed amount to the cost of your treatment. It's normally between £100 and £200 but this can be a very small part of the treatment you get and you normally only pay this once per treatment. If your employer is paying for this cover you will have to pay tax on the cost to them and this should be included in your tax code, a small cost for the peace of mind this cover can bring.

Cash plans

These great plans are generally underused. They provide for smaller, everyday medical costs such as dentists, opticians or physiotherapists. If you have this benefit you can get hundreds of pounds a year paid to cover routine eye tests, glasses, fillings and sometimes even alternative treatments such as massages. Some of these plans also have discount offers on their websites which are worth checking out.

In addition to those valuable benefits, your employer may also offer:

- The option to buy or sell your holiday entitlement
- Childcare vouchers – all parents are entitled to an annual amount of tax-benefited vouchers which can currently save them up to £1,866 jointly per year

- Bikes to Work, helping you to buy a bike tax efficiently and pay for it monthly
- Wills at Work, helping you to spread the cost of buying a will
- Discounts and shopping clubs – if you can save at a place you normally shop it's free money!

Ask your employer about all of these things and get clear on what you are able to receive.

Finally, if you are self-employed, consider which of these benefits you need to provide for yourself.

Outgoings and spending

I blew the budget on a must-have item

I assume you can't take it back? If you can, it's an option!

If the purchase is made, you need a plan to get you back in the black. Firstly, how bad is the debt? How have you paid for it?

If it's overdraft, how will you pay this off? Is there some space in next month's budget? Is it on a credit card? What's the deal on your credit card? Could you reduce the interest or even get an interest free period by switching? Whatever you do, make a plan to pay back the money as soon as possible. The quicker you act, the quicker it can be repaid and the less interest you pay.

> Make a plan to pay back the money as soon as possible

Did you use savings earmarked for something else? And if so was the original target for those savings optional, or not important to you? Or do you need to replace them and if so how quickly?

If you have just opened the bill or statement and reality is hitting home, stop. Take a breath.

Imagine that you already had a plan for how to repay this *must-have-purchase-you-couldn't-live-without*. It would be ok. You blew the budget, but you'll live. You won't be under a bridge, homeless and begging. You'll be safe. You'll kick yourself a little but you've had your notebook out and decided that if you save a bit here, save a bit there, cancel that thing you didn't really want to do, sell some stuff you've never used, after a few months you'll be back in the black.

Oh, you haven't done that yet? Well, what are you waiting for?

My debt is getting out of hand

If your debt means that you can no longer pay your rent or mortgage, buy food or pay bills or if your debt adds up to more than your annual net salary, that's normally a sign you need help. This is the time to act. Don't be scared. Hundreds of thousands of people seek help in the UK for debt problems every year. You will find a list of organisations that can help at the back of this book.

No debt is unsolvable, but the longer you wait, the longer the solution will take. It's not possible to cover all of the possible options here, and everyone is different, but talking to a not-for-profit adviser will help you see ways out of your situation. Time to put on your big brave pants and tackle it. I know someone who had to do this at 21. She was fine by 25, had a family at 29 and moved to her dream home at 33. None of these things would have been possible if she hadn't sought help at the right time.

I'm a shopaholic

We use this as a fun term and there are films and books about shopaholic characters. But a shopaholic is a person *addicted* to shopping. Are you really, actually *addicted*?

The medical term for a shopping addiction is compulsive buying disorder or *oniomania*, from the Greek words *onios* and *manis* – literally 'sale insanity'. Something to think about the next time you're deciding whether to go to the Boxing Day sales?

In an article in Clinical Psychology & Psychotherapy in 2009, Stephen Kellett and Jessica Bolton defined compulsive buying as 'experienced as an irresistible-uncontrollable urge, resulting in excessive, expensive and time-consuming retail activity [that is] typically prompted by negative affectivity' and results in 'gross social, personal and/or financial difficulties'.[11]

Ruth Engs, former professor of Applied Health Sciences at Indiana University, found that some people develop a shopping addiction because shopping triggers the release of happy hormones, endorphins and dopamine. Engs claimed that ten to fifteen percent of the population may be predisposed to these feelings.[12]

If you truly think you are addicted to shopping and experience an uncontrollable urge which is (or probably will end up) causing you difficulty, sadness and debt, can I gently suggest you consult a medical professional? There are many treatments for addictive disorders but for shopping addiction group therapy and cognitive behavioural therapy (CBT) can be very successful. So, stop reading and reach out. You can come back to this book once you've got the personal support you need.

If you're not actually addicted, but use the word

11   Stephen Kellett & Jessica Bolton, Compulsive Buying: A Cognitive-Behavioural Model, Clinical Psychology & Psychotherapy 2009
12   Ruth Engs, How can I manage compulsive shopping and spending addiction? http://www.indiana.edu/~engs/hints/shop.html

shopaholic to excuse and make light of your over-spending here are some tips to help:

- What's your favourite shop? Google its managing director and its board members. Print their pictures. Stick them in your purse. Next time you want to buy something in your favourite shop you will know where the money is going. Perhaps put a picture of you or your loved ones looking happy in there as well. Take a moment to think whether the item will make you, or them, happy?

- Do something else. Instead of going into town shopping go to a green space or beach to clear your head. Take a picnic

- Have some goals. Work towards them every single day. Make something pretty and visual to remind yourself of them and stick it in your purse or wallet

- Allocate treat money. Plan how much of your money you can afford to spend on treats. Aim to stay within that amount and give yourself a pat on the back when you do

- Read a book. Make a pot of tea, curl up on the sofa and escape to someone else's world for a few hours

- Before you hand over your credit or debit card, check your feelings. Are you shopping because you feel sad or happy? Has something happened that made you feel this way? Ask the shop to put the item aside for an hour and go for a walk to review whether it's something you need, can afford, will use and will still love in a week's time

I want to go to the pub

Yes, me too! But what's your budget? If the two drinks in the pub which cost £10 would only cost £2 if you had them at home, could you sit in the garden with them and save £8? Invite friends and get them to bring food and their own drinks.

On the other hand, if you have budgeted for a night in the pub, go and enjoy it. Drink your favourite drink, eat your favourite food and then go home happy. I'm not saying you shouldn't enjoy spending on a night out if you can afford it and the money isn't needed for other things. But if not, maybe the company, the view and the chairs are better at home anyway!

I can't help but buy when I see the emails

Unsubscribe. There is normally a link to this option at the bottom. Or block them. Done. Next!

Shopping is therapy

If it's just now and then, and you can afford it, that's ok. If you use allocated treat money or if you're buying necessities, that's fine.

But if it's to cheer yourself up after an argument with your partner or because you feel sluggish and miserable from a late night, or because you've just received a big credit card bill, spending cash might not help. To be blunt, giving more money to faceless corporations for the latest shiny thing you didn't even know you wanted *It could be time to find another form of therapy* or for a jacket you don't need is not going to make you feel better tomorrow. It might make you happy for ten minutes today, but unless the item is going to bring you joy or be useful for a lot longer, it could be time to find another form of therapy.

To avoid unnecessary spending run through this check-list before you next go shopping:

- Do you really need the items you are going to buy?
- How much joy or value will you get from them?
- Is there money left in your treat budget this month?
- Have you written a list of the shops you'll visit and why you're visiting them?
- Can you get any of the items cheaper online?
- Have you got any discount cards, shopping vouchers, loyalty cards which you can use?
- Is there a shop in which you enjoy browsing but where you often end up spending? How about avoiding it today?
- If you are going to be out shopping for some time, can you take a snack or drink to avoid spending money in coffee shops?

Plan a route to save you time and to stop needless buying, then when you go out:

- If you're driving, take a look at parking charges. Can you set a timer to keep within a parking charge band and keep your trip short?
- Go to the cashpoint and take out what you can afford to spend. Would it help to put it in a separate envelope for each item?

As soon as you get to the shopping centre, take a deep breath, perhaps sit on a bench for a moment and realise what's going on around you. How do the other shoppers look? Are they happy, stressed, loaded-up, energised or tired? How do you feel? Which emotion describes how you feel about this shopping trip? Excited, bored, determined, impatient, nervous or something else? Take note of these and ask yourself if it will help you to achieve shopping success or if it will hinder you. Perhaps visualise yourself sitting on the bench at the end of the shop feeling happy and satisfied, having got what you needed, for a price to fit your budget. Now you can start shopping!

Whilst shopping, don't be influenced by stores' techniques to make you buy. Go in, browse the area that has

Shop smart. Check it's not cheaper online

what you need, try it out and ask questions. Does it really tick the boxes of need or long term joy? Now shop smart. Check it's not cheaper online. Ask the assistant if there any discounts available or if the sale is anytime soon.

Keep these three Vs in mind:

- Vital – you really need this
- Value – it's worth the money (and not just because it has a designer logo)
- Versatile – it will be useful for a decent length of time

Pay for your item(s) and keep your receipt.

Check your feelings again. Are you happy? If not, why not? Is it time for a break, that snack and some thinking time? How long have you got left and does your plan need a revisit?

Before you leave the shopping centre ask yourself if you are still happy with all your purchases? Is there anything you want to take back? It's not too late to do so.

When you get home take pleasure in what went well and the Vital, Valued, Versatile items you bought. Try clothes and shoes on. If you're happy think about when you will wear them.

Put the receipts in a safe place (or in your receipt envelopes if you're tracking outgoings – see "I don't know where my money goes"). If anything is not perfect, put it back in the bag with the receipt, and take it back!

> Remember that everything in shops is designed to make you spend!

Finally, remember that *everything* in shops is designed to make you spend! The lighting, the smell, the music, the layout, the staff, the window, what's on the counter. How many of these can you resist if you go in to a shop? How many of these can you resist if you *don't* go into the shop?

I am usually sensible but go mad when I'm on holiday

Amazing how a touch of sun makes us buy things we would never dream of buying when we are at home isn't it?! Or how juggling currency rates make us frivolous. Or how we buy a handbag or shirt just because it's there.

Set a holiday budget. Book what you can in advance. Plan your travel, insurance, currency buying, car hire, day-to-day expenses. Allocate a set amount of money for treats.

Do some research on what is a good buy where you're going and remember to haggle. Alternatively, just bring home some beautiful photos – they don't cost much to print and will suit your home far better than that gaudy ornament! (If you are going to a far-flung destination where tourism supports the local economy, it might be a nice idea to spend *some* money on souvenirs, but keep it within your budget).

I live in my overdraft

This is really common but the problem is that this is debt like any other. It's possible you will end up using more and more each month, and eventually you could go over your limit, which is when the big charges start. Make today the day you address this.

Take a look at the challenge relating to debt at the end of this book for guidance on how to take control. Can you reduce your outgoings so that you slowly move back into credit? It may take a few months, but it's *so* worth doing.

See also "I blew the budget on a must-have item".

Food takes up all of my money

We have become a nation of foodies with a love of all things food-related – shopping for it, eating it, dining out, fast food, slow food, any food!

But you can control the amount of money you spend on food. There are some great food planners online[13] and lots of books available which are full of cost-effective recipes.[14]

---

13   Try this:
http://www.lovefoodhatewaste.com/content/planning-your-meals-love-food-hate-waste-way
14 https://cookingonabootstrap.com
Try these:
Jack Monroe, A Girl Called Jack, Michael Joseph, 2014
Jamie Oliver, Save with Jamie: Shop Smart, Cook Clever, Waste Less, Michael Joseph, 2013

Other ideas include:

- Do big monthly shops online and buy in bulk. See how long you can go before you have to shop again
- Do not buy food which is on offer unless it is actually cheaper than what you would normally buy
- Shop around and forget brands. Go for taste, seasonality and value for money
- Supermarket wars are still ongoing and the smaller discount supermarkets seem to be winning. Have you tried them? There are online forums which tell you which budget items are as good as the expensive versions.[15]
- It may take a little more time but getting fruit and vegetables from the market, meat from the butcher and only the big stuff from the supermarket could save you hundreds of pounds over time
- Batch cook. When you make a chilli, make three to save time, energy and money
- Have a shelf or space in the fridge labelled 'eat me first'. This stops food waste due to things going past their use-by dates

---

15   *Try these:*
http://www.moneysavingexpert.com/shopping/
https://www.goodhousekeeping.co.uk/institute/food-reviews/food

Take a look at LoveFoodHateWaste.com and Money
Magpie for many more ideas.[16]

Shopping is part of my social life

Are you going shopping with friends or family when
you could do something else less costly? My two friends
Kelly and Sharon often met to go shopping together,
but after the recession hit, they realised they could enjoy
each other's company just as easily by going for a walk,
cooking together, meeting to exercise or even doing
chores together! There is nothing like spending time
with a friend but it can mean that shopping becomes
mindless rather than mindful, and this is when we fall
into unnecessary spending or unhelpful buying.

What could you do rather than shopping? Here are
some free or inexpensive and rewarding ideas:

- **Exercise** – Anything! Walking, running, weights,
  cycling, yoga or choose something else you find fun
- **Cooking** – Cook today's meals, batch cook, make

---

16   *http://www.lovefoodhatewaste.com*
*http://www.moneymagpie.com/save_money_categories/save-money-
shopping*

food as a gift, make sauces, bake a cake for an up-coming celebration

- **Craft** – Make presents, recycle, upcycle, draw something
- **Visit the library** – Take advantage of this free service
- **Chores** – Make them more fun by taking it in turns to help at each other's houses and chat while you clean, decorate or garden
- **TV** – Watch a good film or box set together
- **Skill swap** – Manicure for massage, paperwork for gardening, teaching for DIY? Save money and get stuff done!
- **Volunteer** – Get involved in a cause you care about. Try the National Council for Voluntary Organisations[17] for ideas
- **Music** – Sort out your playlist, your old vinyl or CDs. Make new playlists for different activities

---

17   https://www.ncvo.org.uk/

I go to the supermarket for milk and spend £30!

I hear this a lot from my friends. What is it about a BO-GOF (buy one get one free) offer we can't resist?! Or special offers displayed at the end of every aisle? Did you know that companies pay supermarkets thousands of pounds to have their products placed at the end of aisles? What does that tell you?

Different friends have tried different methods to avoid overspending:

- When Emma goes out for milk, and she only needs milk, she only takes enough money for milk
- Before Joanne goes out for milk she stops and checks what else she may need for the next few days. She makes a list, gets what she needs in one trip and avoids unnecessary multiple shopping trips and the associated opportunities to overspend
- Bridget simply doesn't go. She gets it delivered. You can live without milk if you run out. Have black tea or coffee, toast instead of porridge and tomato based instead of creamy sauces. Place a weekly on-line order. There are no petrol costs and if you don't go to the supermarket you can't spend on extras

Try these ideas out for yourself.

Financial organisations

My credit score is rubbish

Firstly, there is no blacklist as such. However your credit score *does* matter.

Having a higher credit score is vital to securing lower-cost mortgages, credit cards and loans. Making sure yours is as good as it can be is very important, even if you do not need credit at the moment. Checking it at least once a year and improving it if needed is good practice and you can also check that the data held on you is correct. It can also help prevent fraud.

Here are a few tips for improving your score:

- Be on the electoral roll
- Don't have too much open credit that you don't use (unused store or credit cards)
- Have some credit that you pay regularly, on time and in full
- Be on time with all other payments
- Do not take out too many credit agreements in short time periods

- Remember that even applications for credit show up on your record so check your credit rating before you submit applications

You can check your credit score on the following websites:

- **Experian**[18] – Note that there is currently a monthly fee for this after thirty days' usage
- **Noddle**[19] – Note that they recommend credit products too, so use it appropriately
- **MoneySavingExpert.com**[20]– Has a credit club where you can check your credit score but can also help you understand who will lend to you if you need to move debt to a cheaper provider

I don't believe in pensions

Pensions are merely a savings pot for your retirement. You may not understand them or feel they are right for you, but they are just a way of putting money away for your old(er) age, and currently offer some good tax

---

18   http://www.experian.co.uk
19   http://www.noddle.co.uk
20   http://www.moneysupermarket.com

benefits. Also, if you're employed and not in your work-place pension scheme you're turning down free money. See "I don't know what benefits I get from work".

Find out about your current pension(s) today. It's very likely that if you have worked in the UK for a number of years you will be entitled to the state pension. Finding out how much this is and when you will get it will *Find out about your current pension(s) today* help you to build a plan for your retirement. Go to the government's website to check this.[21] And do you have any old pension plans sitting around?

Once you're clear on your current pension situation take some time to consider whether you need to start saving more and, if so, where. The earlier in your life you start this the better. See the Pensions challenge at the end of this book for guidance on how to do this and check out the advice at Money Magpie[22] about how to get the best out of your pension plans.

Also, understand the tax situation. Presently, when you pay into a pension, you get tax relief at your highest rate. This means that the government pays money into your pension when you do. Appreciating this can make

---

21   http://www.gov.uk/check-state-pension
22   http://www.moneymagpie.com/manage_your_money_
categories/pensions

saving for a pension a lot more attractive.

Check where your pension contributions are going. Do you understand where they are invested? Ask your provider or employer to explain. Pensions are invested in a wide variety of funds and you normally get a say in this, depending on your circumstances.

Finally, what are the charges on your pension(s)? Does it make sense to transfer them to an employer's scheme where the charges may be lower? If you have older pensions you might also want to consider moving the funds from those. If you have lost track the government may be able to help you.[23]

Once you understand pensions you may feel more positive about them.

I don't trust banks

Good! You shouldn't, or at least not with everything. As safe places into which your cash is paid they're fine. We all need a place for our money to flow in and out and the government protects the cash you have in banks – see "What if they go bust?" But as far as making financial decisions for you goes? Then you're right not

---

23   https://www.gov.uk/find-pension-contact-details

to trust them. Take responsibility for your own financial decisions yourself, shop around for the best deals or, at the very least, ensure that you understand any advice your bank gives you.

Is your current bank the right one for you? Have you been with them for more than five years, do you have multiple products with them (credit cards, loans, add-on benefits)? Are you happy with the interest you're getting on your accounts and with any charges? Could you get products more cheaply or with better interest?

If you're with one of the big banks do you get what their latest adverts are offering? The best interest rates and benefits are usually only on offer to new customers so compare these to what you, a loyal long-standing customer, are getting. Banks sometimes offer an incentive to switch, which can be worth £100 to £200. It is no longer the difficult process it used to be. £100 for an hour's work? Thank you very much!

I hate insurance companies

Why do you feel like this? If you feel that at some point they negatively affected your financial situation it's probable they were only doing what they were set up to do, which is making money from you, me and everyone else! Any organisation that is set up to make a profit will try to make money from you. Once you accept this it's about how much of your hard-earned cash you are prepared to give them. I suggest you should give away as little

You should give away as little as possible

as possible so it's extremely important that you get the best possible deals.

Ask yourself:

* How long have you been with them?
* Could you pay them annually to save money?
* Do you still need this policy/plan?
* Do they reward your loyalty?
* What about the company's ethics?[24]

Take a look at comparison websites to see if there are better deals with other companies and take a look at the Insurance challenge at the back of this book for more advice.

A word of warning on care: if you're unhappy with cover based on your health risks such as life cover, critical illness cover or permanent health insurance don't cancel it until you are 100% sure you don't need it, or

---

24   *Check out them out at http://www.thegoodshoppingguide.com*

have replaced it with something cheaper or better. As you get older, insurers will normally charge you more. Even if you are offered better rates, wait until a new plan is fully in place before cancelling an old one because from initial quotation to acceptance you may need underwriting which could load your policy with a rating which increases it above the initial quote.

I like to be loyal

How lovely. That's exactly what companies want you to do! The more loyal you are the more profit they make from you. Let's think about how organisations make money. Every time you buy again from an organisation you save them costs. They clearly pass these savings on to you, don't they? Well, no. Test this with one of the financial products you already have. Have you ever actually had a loyalty bonus? If not, ask why, and if there is no incentive for your faithfulness how about considering moving? When you call a provider to say you are leaving because of a better deal they will often match that deal and then it makes sense to remain with them. If they don't, I suggest you need to be loyal to yourself unless their service or product is truly superior to others. Try this with all of the companies you deal with.

Tax...argh!

If you earn money you'll pay it, if you buy something you'll normally pay it and if you die your estate could pay it. Tax is here to stay. If you're employed your employer will pay tax for you and you just have to check your tax code. Doing this means you will not end up owing tax, nor will the tax man end up owing you. Occasionally you can be owed tax and you will not get it back without asking. So it makes sense to know your tax position.

Here's a checklist to help you manage your tax:

- **Check your tax code.** This is vital as it denotes the amount of money you *don't* get taxed on. It gets reduced if you have certain employment benefits or owe money to the tax office. Have a look at the code on your payslip and if necessary ask how it's calculated

- **Check if you can claim tax relief on anything.** The rules on this change regularly but have a chat with your payroll team or an accountant. At present you can claim relief on mileage rates, pensions (depending on how you pay your pension), professional memberships, uniform allowances and charitable gifts. And don't forget marriage allowance

• **Make friends with your payroll team.** They can help explain your tax code, up to a point. They also produce your P60 (an end of year tax form to summarise your tax year) and your P11D (confirming any taxable benefits such as company cars or certain protection plans)

If you've owed tax before, staying on top of tax rules (even though they can be complicated) can help you take control and ensure that this doesn't happen again. Owning or selling shares, owning buy-to-let properties, having certain investments, falling into higher rate tax bands and even child benefit are common reasons for people to be underpaying tax, but there are many more. Self-assessment forms help you identify most of these, but if you miss one, not knowing is not a defence for not paying tax, so it's worth consulting the HMRC's website[25], your payroll department or an accountant.

If you're self-employed or a small business owner

---

25   https://www.gov.uk/government/organisations/hm-revenue-customs

you need a good book-keeper or accountant. Even if it's just to ensure you are in a good state each year. Although they will charge a fee, their advice and processes can normally save you tax and time. If you don't have an accountant ask friends or attend events such as those run by the Federation of Small Businesses to get tips and recommendations.[26]

My student debt worries me

Stop worrying. Don't see UK student debt, via the official student debt channels, as debt.

The rules are subject to change and complex, however you will only pay back this tax on learning once you are earning a certain amount, and even then you will only pay a percentage of the amount over this level. You may never pay all of the debt back. Look up the rules for your scheme and work out how your payments will change if your earnings change. There are calculators online to

Your student loan is intended to push you forward

26   http://www.fsb.org.uk

help.[27] Once you know this, although you will have this outgoing for a very long time, it should feel more like an extra tax and it can help settle you. Never get it confused with debt from credit cards, loans or HP finance. They will hold you back whereas your student loan is intended to push you forward.

---

27   *Try these:*
https://www.gov.uk/repaying-your-student-loan/overview
http://www.moneysavingexpert.com/students/student-finance-calculator
http://www.thecompleteuniversityguide.co.uk/student-loan-repayment-calculator

Other people

My partner/parent does that for me

Brilliant! No time wasted on boring money for you. Marvellous. Except what if they stop or if they are no longer around?

Do you know how much money you have? What happens if you or your partner loses your income? Where are your savings? Are they invested in something safe or a little known gold mine in Guatemala?

Are you protected if you lose your partner, or whoever is looking after your money? A very good friend of mine was left with no money after her partner died suddenly and they had no life cover. She lost her home and her children's father. Then she found a pile of debt and bills. Don't let that be you.

> You need full knowledge of your own financial position

You need full knowledge of your own financial position. Understanding what would happen if you lost your job or if a major financial problem arose tomorrow is the best way of taking control. Also, the stress of relationship changes is bad enough without money complicating it further. Understanding your own money in the good times, means you will be better able to cope during bad times if they happen (and I hope they never do). Consider setting up an emergency fund too.

Just a thought here: how will your partner or parent feel about you wanting to get involved in the management of your own finances? I think it's a good thing to understand. Will they be delighted because they have always wanted you to do it? Or will they feel threatened, insecure, concerned, not trusted or doubtful of your ability? You may need to explain to them why it's important that you start understanding your own money position, and not just because you are afraid they will die! Everyone has different values relating to money. Recognise where you are and where you want to be. This should help the conversation.

If any 'help' or advice doesn't sit well with you, trust your instincts. Nobody can predict the future and anyone who says they can is wrong. When you begin to take control of your money, if questions or objections arise, stand your ground. For example a parent might say, 'But you messed up before' or 'I know better than you'. Have replies ready and be insistent. It's *your* money. If a partner gets angry or hurt this may be more about them and their relationship with you. Separate money issues from relationship issues. If you have concerns about controlling behaviour, talk to someone you trust or get professional help.

My partner only stays with me for my money

There was a great song in the 1980's, 'Ain't nothing going on but the rent' by Gwen Guthrie. Might be worth a listen.

What if the money runs out? If you really want to keep this person you need to manage your cash carefully. But you may also want to talk to Relate[28] or, as a starting point, your friends. Each to their own, but an unequal relationship will fail at some point and then the money side will really get complicated. Consider taking small steps to an equal relationship by dividing up the bills or setting up a joint account into which you both pay money for bills.

---

28   https://www.relate.org.uk/

I am owed money

Go chase it then! If you're owed it you have every right to ask for it back.

If your family owe you money it can be tricky. What was the original arrangement? Did you set a date by which it had to be paid back? Have they missed this? If you don't feel you can ask for the whole sum back immediately what about a payment plan? Don't let your emotions get involved. Be clear and straight forward. If you can afford to be patient, be patient and set a fair, simple schedule. If you didn't set terms be open and ask 'I can't remember what we agreed about paying that cash back, when can you do it?' Be honest and open if you need it back soon.

Don't let your emotions get involved

If you are incurring expenses for your job, record them daily and submit them as often as your employer will allow. If you put things on a credit card for work *you must pay it off!* If you don't have the discipline to do so those little bonus points or air miles are not worth having. Don't kid yourself about the extra money you make on mileage rates – it is not extra money, it goes towards the wear and tear of the business miles on your car. If you get a car allowance, it's for a car. Don't get used to treating this as salary as it will put you in debt! Put it to one side for your next service, replacement tyres or new car.

If you're owed a pay rise when is it due? Have you got it in writing and is it being backdated? Companies are prone to make promises around review times which are then delayed for months whilst approval is sought. Always get any pay promises in writing. Always ask when you will start to receive it and, if you don't, ask for the backdated amount.

You could also check out whether you've ever had a financial product which is now deemed unsuitable, such as PPI (Payment Protection Insurance), as you could get a refund.

> You do not need a special firm to help you claim

You do not need a special firm to help you claim. The Money Advice Service[29] or MoneySavingExpert.com[30] can tell you how to claim. It's well worth checking any mortgage, credit card and loan agreements. If you can see any of the following terms or similar, you've probably been sold PPI:

* Payment cover
* Protection plan

---

29 http://www.moneyadviceservice.org.uk
30 http://www.moneysavingexpert.com

- Loan protection
- Loan care

Even if you can't find the documents it's still worth claiming if you think you were mis-sold PPI. You just need to write to your provider. The Money Advice Service provides template letters on their website. I have many friends who have successfully claimed, for instance Eddie who found when clearing out papers from the loft that he had PPI with several providers from his younger days. He claimed and received £3,000!

I have an adviser who sorts out my money

But do you understand every asset you have, and the point of it? Do you know what you are paying in charges and if that's reasonable? Will your investments be flexible enough to allow for changes in your circumstances?

Even if your adviser is a friend, even if you have used them forever and they advised your Dad when television was still black and white, at your next review meeting ask questions. Ask the 'what if' questions, ask if you're in a good place, why you have the investment(s), if it's the best value and the tax position. If it's a pension ask if it is enough to provide for you in retirement. Ask if you should reduce your mortgage. Think of as many questions as you can and ask them. Ask again if you don't understand. A good adviser

Ask if you're in a good place

will be willing to project your cash flow and position in future years so you know where you stand.

If you are not happy with your adviser ask friends and colleagues for recommendations or look at Unbiased's downloadable checklist.[31]

Organisation

I'm so disorganised and the paperwork just builds up

Having disorganised bills and paperwork means that you can easily miss payment dates and then end up paying extra charges. So you need a system.

I use a ring binder and pretty dividers. You could do the same or use a concertina file or scan paperwork and store it on your laptop (making sure you back it up). There are apps now which turn photos of your receipts into documents for filing. Find something which works for you.

You could sort your paperwork into the following sections:

* Important documents – birth and marriage certificates, passports, etc
* Mortgage or rent
* Council tax
* Utilities
* Insurance – home, car, life, health, travel etc
* Car related documents
* Savings – bank, ISAs, bonds, etc

- Bank statements (only keep the last few and if you bank online you only need your annual interest statement or a note of your accounts)
- Borrowing – credit cards, loans, HP, etc
- Pensions
- Tax
- Receipts for big or important items

Keeping it in a folder or two like this means you can always locate the latest bill or notice. I normally bin a statement each time a new one comes in (as long as I have no disputes or queries) so that the paper doesn't accumulate.

If you have a smartphone you might want to use the calendar to set reminders for what has to be paid and when. You can also schedule payments from your bank account ahead of time.

It only has to be done once

If you're feeling disorganised this might sound daunting, but it only has to be done *once*. After that you'll have a system which will take minimum maintenance if you deal with each piece of paper when it arrives.

I lose track of my money

Looking at what's in your bank account doesn't always help. You need to remember what else has to come out and when, as you may have a big expense coming up which you could have forgotten about. To help with this I would suggest the money pots method.

You may remember a parent or grandparent dividing cash between pots or envelopes when you were small. With the advent of bank cards, internet banking and contactless payments we've stopped doing this, but it was useful. Consider setting up a separate bank account in which you can save money for bills. You could then have other named savings accounts into which you can transfer regular or one-off amounts to pay for short or longer term commitments. I currently have accounts called Christmas, Car and Girls Away. These are not my long term savings accounts but Christmas comes every year so putting away an amount every month means when I go shopping in November I have money saved to cover it. When my car needs taxing, insuring or fitting with tyres the £100 per month I have put away covers the cost. Girls Away is my fun account for my annual trip with friends.

The benefit of this approach is that you always have the money you need. Plus you can look at your current account and know what unallocated money is left.

No more losing track! What do you want or need to save for? What will you call your accounts?

I can't find the time to organise my money

Yes, it does take time. But what is it you need to do? This is all about what's important to you. Make a list of everything you need to address, prioritise the tasks, then set yourself a target of ticking off one per week. The challenges at the back of this book will show you how.

Sometimes it's even worth scheduling a day's holiday from work to get this stuff done, without interruption, because once it's done it's easier to stay on top of it.

Or consider this: how much do you earn per hour or per day? Work it out.

Let's say you earn £25,000:
£25,000 ÷ 52 weeks = £480 per week
£480 ÷ 35 hours = £13.74 per hour

Is it worth the value of your time to take an hour or a day off to do what you need to do? Maybe you could use some paid holiday?

If you can get a £100 reward for changing your

bank account then a day off would be paid for. You could also save £100 or more in a day by cutting costs relating to debt, credit cards and utility bills.

I know I should get organised but there's always something that needs my money

Yes, there always will be and that's why having a plan and budgeting is so vital. A rigorous review of everything you spend can help you identify patterns and problem areas and help you to predict when you might need money for what would otherwise be unexpected expenses. This will take the stress down a few levels and reduce panic and impulses which might damage your situation further. The other potential upside is that you might find that you have more money than you thought which you can use to fund things you've always wanted to do or buy, or to give you more stability.

So when is a good time for you to do this? Take an hour now to get it started and book an hour next week to continue. After a few hours over a few months you should get it down to just a few minutes per week. See the Outgoings challenge at the end of this book for a suggestion on how to do this.

The future

I'll never have any money

If you have a job and you get paid each month, you have money. Every month. What you do with it is your choice. Yes, you need somewhere to live, you need to keep warm and eat and you may have dependents you need to care for. But you are in control of this. Having money is about having enough to cover your needs.

Sometimes you will have difficulties and lean periods but when these happen thinking calmly about how to tackle the situation is much better than presuming the worst.

Get clear on your outgoings and on whether they can be reduced. You might free up some extra money. Also, double check your benefit entitlement. The benefit calculators from the Citizens Advice Bureau[32] or EntitledTo[33] might be helpful.

Writing down what you *do* have at the moment

---

32   https://www.citizensadvice.org.uk/benefits/
33   http://www.entitledto.co.uk

and then making plans to add small amounts when you can could improve the way you feel. Small achievements will lead to bigger ones. What can you do today? Also, acknowledge the non-financial assets you have – not just possessions but family, friends, home, job and a smile.

Keep your finances tidy, be careful with your outgoings and start building some savings. Everyone starts somewhere.

I could be dead tomorrow and you can't take it with you

I am not going to give the statistics on the likelihood of you dying tomorrow but trust me, it's not likely. You are likely to live into your mid-80s. So actually whilst you *could* be dead tomorrow it's much more likely you'll live for a long time yet. This means, on average, over twenty years of retirement and for some it could be over thirty. For some people, particularly those that have taken a career break, this could be more years than they actually worked!

Now, whilst it's a good idea to plan for dying tomorrow (life cover, a will, etc) for peace of mind and for those you care for, it's much more important to plan for the long term. You can still have fun but you'll have it for longer if you plan properly.

What are your goals and dreams? What do you want to have achieved when you reach 80 or beyond, and what memories would you like to have? Use these things as motivation to plan and save for a long life, so you are able to afford them when you don't drop dead tomorrow.

My savings are for a rainy day

Well done on having some savings!

But always ask questions of your savings to make sure they are working as hard as they can. Are they tax efficient? Have you used this year's tax allowances? Are you being too loyal to an old account? Is the interest rate as good as you can get? What is this money for?

If you have debts as well as savings having savings might not be a good idea. Are you charged more interest on your debts than you earn on your savings? I see it so many times. Someone has a £3,000 credit card debt on which they are charged 26% interest and £3,000 in savings on which they are earning 2%. Having savings may make you feel rich, but it's usually better to use them to pay off debts. And if that rainy day comes along you can always use the credit card (when you've found one with an interest free period)!

I'm hoping for an inheritance

When? You can't know when someone will die, nor if they will actually leave you anything.

If it's your parents' pension or estate you're thinking about, how old will you be? What happens if they live to be a hundred? Or live for twenty years longer than you think they will and need to pay for long-term care?

You can't be sure of when or if you will inherit anything so take control of your finances now. And then if you do inherit it will be a lovely bonus.

Next Steps

I've made numerous references to challenges through-out this book, so here they are.

They are intended to help you gather your thoughts about where you are now and then give guidance on how to take control of things and get on the right path for the future.

When I run these challenges as workshops it's great to see the lightbulb moment when people realise that they *can* make progress with money and that it will af-fect their whole life in a positive way.

Challenge one – income
Understand what you have coming in

How do you feel about what you earn? Do you compare it to what others earn, or to the past or the future? What about the deductions? How do you feel on payday? Just spending five minutes exploring this can bring out some interesting points, which may be correct or may be incorrect, but they set the scene for this challenge.

Next what's your objective here? What do you need to do to be comfortable with what you have coming in, and to understand it? Examples might include understanding your payslip or employee benefits if you're employed or being able to predict your cashflow if you're self-employed. It must be your personal plan.

Then, plan how you are going to achieve that. Break it down into tasks. For instance, if you want to understand your payslip the tasks might be:

- Print off payslip and take a look at each element
- Check tax code
- Visit HR department with questions

Finally, review this regularly – put a diary note on your calendar or in your phone for the next time you need to review.

Challenge two – outgoings
Understand what you have going out

First, think about how you feel about where your money goes at the moment. All of your thoughts and feelings are valid here. Identifying the things on which you are happy to spend money and the things which annoy you can help you get better with money. Which expenses really annoy you? What do you feel happy about paying for? For instance, I love my home so am happy to pay my mortgage but I hate food shopping. I am happy with my gym subscription but wish I had never bought the car as the finance payments are painful. This exercise might just get some of the negative thinking out of the way and help you move forward.

Next, what is your objective for improving the way you manage your outgoings? It might be:

- I want to feel more in control (If so, what does that mean for you?)
- I want to pay all my bills on time
- I want to ensure that I am not paying more than I need to
- I want to start saving
- I don't want to buy impulsively

If you have more than one take one at a time. What are the tasks involved? For instance, if your objective is to ensure you're not paying more than you need the tasks might be:

- Gather bills together
- Take a look at comparison websites for each of them to see if a different provider would offer a better deal
- Make the switch

Then set a review date. This might be monthly or weekly depending on your goal. You might want to include a

reward here for dealing with the hard, boring stuff –
make it non-financial if you can!

Challenge three – debt
Take control of your debt

Debt in the UK is epidemic. If you are in debt you are
not alone, but you need to put together a plan to reduce it. I am not talking mortgages here, but personal
debt: overdrafts, credit cards, store cards, catalogue and
mail order accounts, hire purchase, car finance, personal loans and payday loans.

Allow yourself to acknowledge how you feel about
your debt. Debt is common, so don't beat yourself up.
This may be the hardest of these challenges as debt can
feel so overwhelming but there is a lot of help available
to get you back on track.

Your first objective should be to understand your
debt. Having it written down in one place can be a
shock but without knowing what it looks like you cannot tackle it. You can use the one page budget planner
at the end of this book.

Your steps for moving forward could then be:

* Contact lenders to see if interest rates can be reduced

- Review other outgoings to see if you can make savings elsewhere
- Contact a debt charity for help and support

Or:
- Move biggest debt(s) to an interest free credit card
- Work out how much needs to be paid each month to pay it off before the interest free term ends
- Understand if this is affordable and set a date to review it three months before the term ends

Or:
- Get credit rating
- Close any credit that's not used or which has a high interest rate
- Work to improve credit rating
- Apply for loan with a lower interest rate to help clear current debts

Your plan is *your* plan. It will vary for each person and their situation. But start with three steps and tick them off one by one. And get appropriate help. Don't wait, do it today. It will take time, and getting out of debt is not easy but it is possible and the sooner you start the sooner it will be over.

Challenge four – cushions
Build emergency funds and financial resilience

Cushions?! Not the thing you throw on your sofa but a financial cushion to protect you from life's ups and downs. A cushion in money form, that doesn't shield you from difficulties but provides the padding to help you spring back when something unexpected happens and you need some cash.

What are your immediate thoughts? Have you got a cushion? How do you feel about having an emergency fund or not having one? Take five minutes to explore this and write down how you feel. Think about a situation which would involve an unexpected expense. Think of that situation if you had no money put away, then think of it if you had an emergency fund of, say, £1,000. Having an emergency fund would take some stress out of the situation.

Before you read on *you cannot do this until you have your debt in hand. I repeat....do the debt challenge first!* Also, if you have easy-access savings, you may decide you don't need the emergency fund as well (just remember to have a plan to replace your savings after any emergency).

If you need to build a cushion your plan might be:

- Decide how much you need, but don't worry too much about this – any cushion is better than none!
- Direct a certain amount to your emergency fund monthly or try putting a few pounds away in a tin every day or week then banking it
- Store your cushion in an easy access account with the best interest rate you can find

Learn to value the 'springiness' your cushion can give you, and feel good about it. And if you need to use it for a crisis or difficulty remember to start rebuilding as soon as you can. But also pat yourself on the back for having had it available!

Challenge five – home
Don't pay more than you need to for your home

If you currently have a mortgage how do you feel about it? Is it manageable? Do you know the facts about it – the interest rate, the review date? How and when you will pay it off? Will you pay it off?

If you don't yet have a mortgage how do you feel about that? Have you had a good or bad experience renting? Do you have a realistic plan to get on the housing ladder? Do you find mortgages scary or confusing?

Next, what's your objective? If it's switching to a better mortgage rate your tasks might be:

- Complete budget planner at the back of this book to understand what you can afford to pay
- Check credit rating
- Understand current mortgage
- Contact lender for current offers
- Consult mortgage adviser for offers from other lenders
- Take action accordingly

If you don't yet have a mortgage but want to get on the property ladder, your tasks might be:

- Complete budget planner at the back of this book to understand what you can afford to pay
- Check credit rating
- Check home buying options
- Work out plan to get the necessary deposit (the budget planner will help you to identify any spare cash)
- Consult mortgage adviser
- Take action accordingly

Whichever tasks are relevant, it is vital to ensure your credit record is in a good place before you start.

And when you've achieved a better mortgage rate, or got your first mortgage, remember to set a date to check your progress on repayments, review home expenses and current mortgage rates.

Challenge six – insurance
Protecting what's important to you

Insurance products can be confusing. Do you need every type of insurance even if you could afford them all? Unlikely! However, spending your hard-earned cash on the policies you need the most is vital.

Your objective here is to be able to sleep at night. So what keeps you awake? What are your main worries and what are your biggest risks? Acknowledge that you will never claim on some policies but some will be there in your biggest hour of need. Then set your priorities. Questions for you:

- What do you need?
- Who or what does it cover?
- What do you have already?
- What does your employer provide?

- How long is it since you checked the market?
- Are your nomination forms (for beneficiaries) up to date?
- Do you have a will?

Ask for advice if you need it. Speak to an adviser, use the Money Advice Service[34] or look at comparison sites. Understand what you have and why. Write them down in order of the value you place on them. This will change as life changes. For instance, when you're young, you couldn't care less about life insurance but as you get older and have more responsibilities you'll value the help it would give your dependents if the worst happened.

Then set yourself tasks to review each of your insurance policies and make your informed decisions about what to do with each. Lastly, set a reminder to review this again.

Challenge seven – pensions
Providing for your own future

Saving for retirement starts with you believing that one day you will be old. The odds of you getting old are

---

34   http://www.moneyadviceservice.org.uk

good. Should you actually die before you get there any money you save in a pension can benefit your loved ones but the big problem, if you want to see it that way, is that most of us will live to be in our mid-80s and one in three of those born in 2013 will make it to 100. If one of those people gave up work at 65 they'd have 35 years in retirement – hence the need to start saving in a pension scheme early!

How do you feel about saving for retirement? It's interesting that once people hit a 'big' age like 30, 40 or 50 they want to discuss and think about pensions whereas in reality, the amounts you save before 30 have the biggest effect on your pension pot because you have saved them for the longest. You shouldn't normally opt out of a workplace scheme as most UK employers are now made to contribute so these are usually a good deal and the worst thing you can do is ignore pensions altogether.

To understand and improve your pension position your tasks could be:

- Find out about state pension entitlement
- Get forecast for any other current pensions
- Find out where pensions are invested and decide whether you are happy with that
- Work out what you will need in retirement
- Consider whether you need to save more

- Check if you are paying enough into your workplace pension in order to get the highest contribution from your employer
- Check you are receiving or claiming tax relief at your highest level or paying via salary sacrifice[35] if it's available

Pensions don't need to be reviewed quite as often as other money matters but put a review date in your diary or phone anyway so that you don't forget. It's Pensions Awareness Day on 16th September each year so is that a good day?

Challenge eight – savings
Saving what you need to fund your goals

Focusing on what you are saving for can make it much more achievable. So what would you like to save money for? What's your motivation? Why is it so important? You might want a new car next year, or are planning to get married, or want to save money for your children's future. Whatever it is, your tasks for setting up a savings habit would probably look like this:

---

35   See https://www.gov.uk/guidance/salary-sacrifice-and-the-effects-on-paye for an explanation

- Write down goals and place them somewhere visible
- Check budget (use the planner at the end of this book)
- Check interest rates on existing savings accounts or shop around for the best ones and open a new account
- Set up regular automated standing order to a savings account or ISA
- Set short, mid and long term goals for how much you want to have saved

Then ensure that you set a date to review.

Budget Planner

WHAT'S COMING IN?

Income

Salary	£
One-offs	£
Other	£

Total coming in £

Employer benefits

Pension	£
Life cover	£
Other	£

WHAT'S GOING OUT?

Regular expenses

Rent/mortgage	£
Council tax	£
Gas/electricity	£
Water	£
Mobile phone	£
TV licence	£
Broadband/TV/landline	£
Car (tax/insurance/MOT/repairs)	£
Insurance	£
Food	£
Family costs	£
Clothing (essential)	£
Savings	£
Other	£
TOTAL	**£**

DEBTS

Credit cards	£
Loans	£
Other	£
TOTAL	**£**

Day to day expenses

Lunches/food/drinks	£
Travel	£
Other	£
TOTAL	**£**

Savings ideas	The good stuff	
Review rate?	Gym	£
Any rebates due?	Socialising	£
Try switching?	Clothing (non-essential)	£
Is this the best deal?	Holidays	£
	Gifts	£
Is this the best deal?	Birthdays/Christmas	£
	Hobbies	£
	Memberships	£
Make a weekly menu plan?	Other	£
	TOTAL	**£**
	Total going out	**£**

PUTTING IT TOGETHER	
Total coming in	**£**
Total going out	**£**
What's left?	**£**

Some Final Thoughts

When it comes to money we are all different. We can earn the same pay, be the same age, live in the same town and have the same parents but none of these things mean we will have the same level of wealth or financial stability. That depends on what we do with the money we receive, which in turn is often governed by the upbringing we have had, our culture, our experiences and how we feel at any given moment. No wonder we sometimes struggle. Think of every money experience you have ever had: your pocket money, hearing your parents talk about money, your first pay packet or bill, the times you had no money, the times you had lots of money, splurges, unpaid bills, breaking into your piggy bank, losing your bank card. All of these things will have affected your financial decision making and subsequent financial fitness. But we can all get better with money.

Being better with money is not something you can fake or make up but it is something which will help you for the rest of your life. It means that money is not the issue when a problem happens. It means you are in control. There may be difficult times but if you are better with money you will be able to pause, breathe and plan your way out of the situation.

For the future, understand that making one mistake doesn't mean you need to make another one. Get help when you need it. Revisit the advice in this book if you need to, or if you hear yourself making an excuse. We British are not big on talking about money but I've always found that once we start we often can't be stopped! A lack of education and some common misconceptions shouldn't stop us trying to be better and other people will want to share and help. If this book has helped you or you think it might help someone else please pass it on.

Ask questions, do your research, use unbiased websites, get organised

Every day is a new day. Every financial decision is a chance to practise being better with money. You can do this. Make sure you believe that. If you do not believe, *pretend* you do. Eventually you will start to believe and it will come more naturally. Remember – ask questions, do your research, use unbiased websites, get organised. There is no money issue that cannot be solved with a deep breath and the right information and guidance. Do it. Do it today.

About the author

Jo Thresher is an award-winning financial services professional and money coach with a true understanding of the difference between what people need and what typical financial service providers tell them.

With almost thirty years' experience in the industry Jo set up her own financial education business Better With Money with the aim of helping everyone to improve their financial wellbeing. Jo's business helps large and small businesses in the UK to educate their employees on money matters: from debt and budgeting to wills and pensions and everything in between. Jo's system of challenges and workshops has been highly successful in moving people forward to a better financial place without being boring or selling products. Jo's aim is to rid the workplace of financial stress.

Jo is originally from Essex but now lives in Bristol with her husband, children and her parents.

Find out more at:
www.betterwithmoney.com
Twitter – @jothresherjo

Acknowledgements

Thank you to my fantastic husband Paul and children Louis, Ruby, Rhys and Owain. You're priceless to me. To my lovely Mum & Dad who cared for me and my amazing siblings Louise, Ed & Neil. Big families mean you have to be better with money!

Behind every happy person are tribes who have helped to support them. In my working life it was Alan Stevenson and the Dream Team, Beach, Geoff and Craig. In my family life my mummy group – Jo, Emma, Kelly, Helen, Sharon, Caroline, Elaine and Becca. For proofreading my eagle-eyed special friend Bridget Bennett (and wine and Benshers). In helping me develop the courage to be me it was my fantastic tribe Kelly, Lindsay, Helene and Jane. For the courage and support you gave me to set up my business Better with Money Ltd a huge thank you to Katy Forsyth, Alex Alway, Emily Degan, Katie Vye and Vanessa Brock.

Thanks also to all the great clients I have worked with especially Michelle, Stacy and Richard at Admiral – you inspired this work and your encouragement, suggestions, stories and time really helped.

Lastly thanks to the lovely Amanda Cullen for introducing me to the wonderful publisher Joanne Henson.

This book is dedicated to the memory of Emma Wy-gladala.

Reference/
bibliography

References

Ruth Engs, *How can I manage compulsive shopping and spending addiction?*
http://www.indiana.edu/~engs/hints/shop.html

The Guardian, *Austerity a Factor in Rising Suicide Rate Among UK Men*
https://www.theguardian.com/society/2015/nov/12/austerity-a-factor-in-rising-suicide-rate-among-uk-men-study

David Gunnell, Jenny Donovan, Maria Barnes, Rosie Davies, Keith Hawton, Nav Kapur, Will Hollingworth, Chris Metcalfe, *The 2008 Global Financial Crisis: effects on mental health and suicide*
http://www.bris.ac.uk/media-library/sites/policybristol/documents/PolicyReport-3-Suicide-recession.pdf

Stephen Kellett & Jessica Bolton, *Compulsive Buying: A Cognitive-Behavioural Model,* Clinical Psychology & Psychotherapy 2009

Jack Monroe, *A Girl Called Jack*, Michael Joseph, 2014

Jamie Oliver, *Save with Jamie: Shop Smart, Cook Clever, Waste Less*, Michael Joseph, 2013

StepChange Debt Charity, *Becoming a Nation of Savers*
https://www.stepchange.org/Portals/0/documents/Reports/BecominganationofsaversStepChangeDebtCharityreport.pdf

Useful websites

All round help
http://www.moneyadviceservice.org.uk
http://www.moneymagpie.com
http://www.moneysavingexpert.com

Benefits entitlement
https://www.citizensadvice.org.uk/benefits/
http://www.entitledto.co.uk

Credit card repayments
https://www.moneyadviceservice.org.uk/en/tools/credit-card-calculator

Credit checking

http://www.experian.co.uk

http://www.noddle.co.uk

http://www.moneysupermarket.com

Debt

www.citizensadvice.org.uk

www.capuk.org

www.stepchange.org

www.payplan.com

www.nationaldebtline.org

Financial advisers

https://www.unbiased.co.uk/

http://www.fsb.org.uk

Financial Services Compensation Scheme

https://www.the-fca.org.uk/consumers/claim-compensation-firm-fails

Help to buy a home

https://www.helptobuy.gov.uk

Money making ideas

http://www.moneymagpie.com

http://www.moneysavingexpert.com

Mortgage calculators

https://www.moneyadviceservice.org.uk/en/tools/mort-gage-calculator
http://www.moneysavingexpert.com/mortgages/mort-gage-rate-calculator

Pensions

http://www.gov.uk/check-state-pension
https://www.gov.uk/find-pension-contact-details
http://www.thegoodshoppingguide.com
http://www.moneymagpie.com/manage_your_money_categories/pensions

Relationship issues

https://www.relate.org.uk/

Salary sacrifice

https://www.gov.uk/guidance/salary-sacrifice-and-the-effects-on-paye

Saving on food

http://www.lovefoodhatewaste.com/content/planning-your-meals-love-food-hate-waste-way
https://cookingonabootstrap.com
http://www.moneymagpie.com/save_money_catego-ries/save-money-shopping

Smart Energy GB

www.smartenergygb.org

Student debt

https://www.gov.uk/repaying-your-student-loan/over-view

http://www.moneysavingexpert.com/students/student-finance-calculator

http://www.thecompleteuniversityguide.co.uk/student-loan-repayment-calculator

Tax

https://www.gov.uk/government/organisations/hm-revenue-customs

Volunteering

https://www.ncvo.org.uk/

Other recommended reading

Alvin Hall, *You and Your Money*, Hodder, 2006

Martin Lewis, *The Three Most Important Lessons You've Never Been Taught*, Vermillion, 2008

Karen Pine & Simonne Gnessen, *Sheconomics*, Headline, 2009

Index

A

Advice online is confusing   41
Adviser sorts out my
    money   108
Attitude and beliefs   **55**

B

Bad news, I might discover   38
Banks, I don't trust   94
Bed, I'll just keep it under
    the   38
Beliefs   **55**
Benefits
    employee   70
    workplace   70
Benefits of being better
    with money   26
Blew the budget   75
Bills just stack up   51
Boring, sorting out money is 55
Budget, blew   75
Budget planner   **137**
Bust, what if they go?   35

C

Can't help but buy when I
    see the emails   81
Citizens Advice Bureau   117

Confusing
    advice online   41
    it's all too   42
Consequences of not being
    better with money   80
Credit card
    is my friend   58
Credit score is rubbish   91
Cushions challenge   128

D

Debt
    everyone's in   63
    is getting out of hand   76
    student   100
Debt challenge   126
Disorganised   111
Don't believe in pensions   92
Don't know where my
    money goes   43
Don't trust banks   94
Don't want to know   56

E

Earned it, I   61
Emails   81
Engs, Ruth   78
EntitledTo   117

Erratic income   68
Experian   92

F
Fears   **35**
Federation of Small
   Businesses   100
Financial organisations   **91**
Financial Services
   Compensation Scheme   35
Food takes up all of my
   money   86
Future   **117**

H
Help to Buy   53
Holiday, go mad when I
   am on   85
Home   **45**
Home challenge   129
Home, I'll never be able to
   afford my own   53

I
Income   **65**
Income challenge   123
Income is erratic   68
Interest rates, on mortgage   49
Inheritance   120
Insurance challenge   131
Insurance companies   95

K
Kellett & Bolton, Stephen
   & Jessica   78

Know, don't want to   56
Knowledge   **41**

L
Losing track of money   113
Loyalty   97
LoveFoodHateWaste.com   88

M
Money Advice Service   41, 59
Money Magpie   88, 93, 107
MoneySavingExpert.com
                       41, 92, 107
Mortgages   45

N
National Council for
   Voluntary Organisations   89
No money to manage   65
No one taught me   42
Noddle   92
Not paid enough   67

O
Online advice is confusing   41
Organisation   **111**
Organised, I know I should
   get   115
Other people   **103**
Outgoings and spending   **75**
Outgoings challenge   124
Overdraft   85
Owed money   106

P
Paperwork builds up 111
Parent looks after my
    money 103
Partner
    looks after my money 103
    only stays with me for
    my money 105
Past **31**
Payment protection
    insurance 107
Pensions
    don't believe in 92
Pensions challenge 132
Plenty of income, so what
    if I waste some? 66
Pub, I want to go to the 80

R
Rainy day 119
Relate 105
Ripped off, I've been 33
Risky, it's all too 36
Rubbish credit score 91
Rubbish with money 31, 62

S
Savings challenge 134
Screwed up big time in the
    past 32
Shopaholic 77
Shopping
    is part of my social life 88
    is therapy 81

Social life, shopping is
    part of 88
Sorting out money is boring 55
Spending **75**
StepChange Debt Charity 24
Student debt 100
Supermarket, I go to for
    milk and spend £30 90

T
Tax…argh 98
Therapy, shopping is 81
Tight, people who care too
    much about money are 57
Time, lack of 114
Too young to worry about
    money 64

U
Unbiased.co.uk 109
Under the bed, keeping it 38

W
Work and income **65**
Workplace benefits 70
Worth it, I'm 60

Y
Young, too 64

Also in this series

What's Your Excuse for not Eating Healthily?

Joanne Henson
Overcome your excuses and eat well to look good and feel great

Do you wish you could eat more healthily and improve the way you look and feel, but find that all too often life gets in the way? Do you regularly embark on healthy eating plans or diets but find that you just can't stick with them? Then this is the book for you.

This isn't another diet book. Instead it's a look at the things which have tripped you up in the past and offers advice, ideas and inspiration to help you overcome those things this time around.

No willpower? Hate healthy food? Got no time to cook? Crave sugary snacks? Overcome all of these excuses and many more. Change your eating habits and relationship with food *for good*.

Paperback – ISBN 978-0-9933388-2-3
e-book – ISBN 978-0-9933388-3-0

Also in this series

What's Your Excuse for not Living a Life You Love?

Monica Castenetto
Overcome your excuses and lead a happier, more fulfilling life

Are you stuck in a life you don't love? Have you reached a point where your life doesn't feel right for you anymore? Then this book is for you.

This is not yet another self-help book claiming to reveal the secret to permanent happiness. Instead, it helps you to tackle the things which have been holding you back and gives ideas, advice and inspiration to help you move on to a better life.

Don't know what you want? Scared of failure? Hate change? Worried about what others might think? This book will help you overcome all of your excuses and give you the motivation you need to change your life.

Paperback – ISBN 978-0-9933388-4-7
e-book – ISBN 978-0-9933388-5-4

Also in this series

What's Your Excuse for not Loving Your Job?

Amanda Cullen
Overcome your excuses and change the way you feel about your work

Do you have a job which you're not enjoying as much as you know you should? Do you dread Mondays, spend your free time worrying about your work or feel undervalued by your boss or colleagues? If so, this book is for you.

In this supportive and motivational book Amanda Cullen takes a look at the wide variety of excuses we use which keep us stuck and unhappy in our work. She offers ideas and advice on how to tackle issues so that you can take control, make the necessary changes and transform your working life.

Don't like your colleagues? Spend too long in the office? Not confident in your skills? Or just plain bored? Overcome all of these and many more, and learn how to love your job.

Paperback – ISBN 978-0-9933388-6-1
e-book – ISBN 978-0-9933388-7-8

Also in this series

What's Your Excuse for not Getting Fit?

Joanne Henson
Overcome your excuses and get active, healthy and happy

Do you want to be fit, lean and healthy, but find that all too often life gets in the way? Do you own a gym membership you don't use, or take up running every January only to give up in February? Then this is the book for you.

This is not yet another get-fit-quick program. It's a look at the things which have prevented you in the past from becoming the fit, active person you've always wanted to be, and a source of advice, inspiration and ideas to help you overcome those things this time around. Change your habits and attitude to exercise for good.

Too tired? Lacking motivation? Bored by exercise? You won't be after reading this book!

Paperback – ISBN 978-0-9933388-0-9
e-book – ISBN 978-0-9933388-1-6